My name is Lana.
What is your name? ____________________

Jennifer Moore-Mallinos / Marta Fàbrega

I CAN'T HEAR VERY WELL

Hi! My name's Lana, I'm ten years old and I'm deaf. That means my ears don't work very well, so I can't hear like other people can. Some people whose ears are like mine might say that they're hard of hearing or hearing impaired. No matter which way you say it, they both mean that a person has trouble hearing. Some people can hear a little and some not at all.

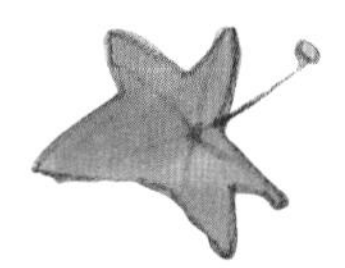

30
30

I HAVE FUN

Being deaf doesn't mean that I can't do all the things that other kids my age can do, and it doesn't mean that I can't have fun either. I love to play sports—especially volleyball! I even made the team at my school. I love to read and play video games too! And just like other kids, I have to keep up with my school work. The only thing I can't do very well is hear.

A REALLY QUIET WORLD

Have you ever wondered what it would be like if you couldn't hear anything at all or could only hear just a little bit? Just think how quiet it would be!
For us, the world is definitely a lot quieter than it is for most people, but there are some ways to break the silence.

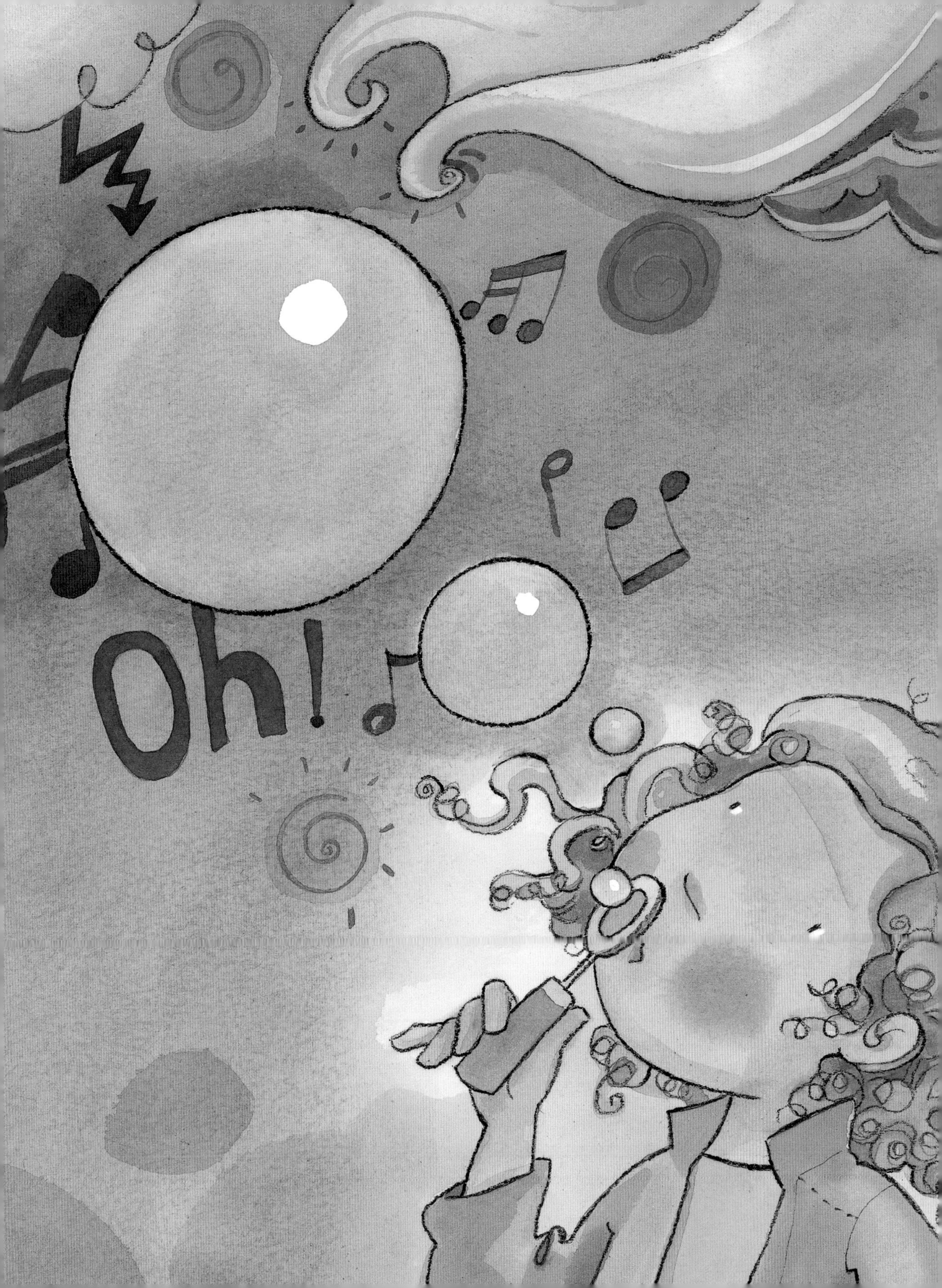
Oh!

A LITTLE DEVICE BEHIND MY EAR

Just like a lot of other kids who have trouble hearing, I wear a hearing aid. My hearing aid fits perfectly around my ear, and it's so small that you can barely see it. Some kids have hearing aids that fit inside their ear like a tiny earbud, and others might even have invisible hearing aids that fit deep in their ear canal. My hearing aid is really good at helping me hear some sounds.

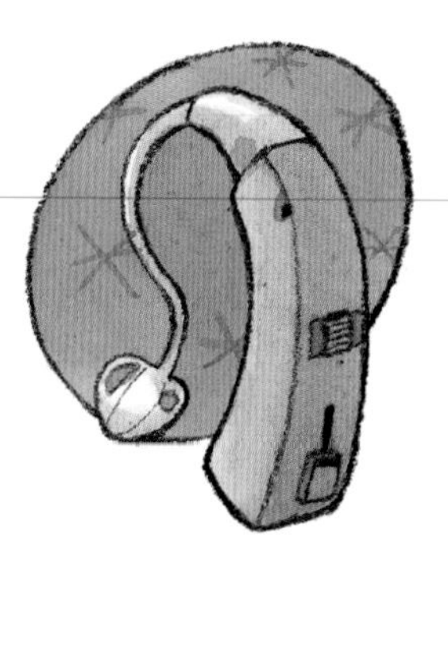

I wear my hearing aid all the time
except when I go swimming or to bed.
At school, my teacher, Mrs. Langley,
wears a small microphone around her
neck that helps me hear her better.
And when she speaks, she always makes
sure she talks slowly and is facing me.
Mrs. Langley can also have what she's
saying put into words that I can read on a
screen. Being deaf is not going to get in
the way of my learning!

HOORAY FOR TECHNOLOGY!

There are some other kids in my school who are deaf or hard of hearing just like me. At recess we like to hang out together and speak with our hands—it's called sign language. Using sign language to talk with my friends is fun because it's a special language we can use to communicate with each other. Have you ever seen a person use sign language to communicate?

THE BODY LANGUAGE

Sign language is not only for deaf people. Other people who aren't deaf can learn how to sign, too!
Just like many other things, learning how to use sign language takes practice. When we talk in sign language, we say we are "signing." When I sign, I use my hands to make different shapes that mean certain things. I also use my face and my body to help me communicate how I'm feeling.

NOW WE HAVE A NEW CLUB!

When the other kids at school first saw us communicating with each other using sign language, they were fascinated. That's when I had a great idea!

With Mrs. Langley's help, we started a sign language club. We couldn't believe how many kids wanted to learn how to sign. So every morning, we help Mrs. Langley teach the other kids how to sign. Now during recess, instead of the other kids watching us sign, we all communicate together.

LOOKING AT PEOPLE'S MOUTHS

Not everybody who is deaf or hearing impaired knows sign language. Some people can read lips! That means that they can see what a person is saying by the way they are moving their lips. It takes a long time to learn how to read lips, and so far I'm doing pretty good. But I still have a lot to learn. Just think how much fun I have when I can see what the kids on the playground are saying, no matter where I am standing!

USING OUR EYES INSTEAD

There are a lot of really neat things that help people who are deaf. Some people have special telephones that light up instead of ringing. And then instead of hearing the conversation, the telephone types out the message on a screen, and the person can read what is being said. How cool is that!

DOGS NOT ONLY HELP BLIND PEOPLE...

I'm lucky because I have a hearing dog named Barkley. Barkley's job is to let me know if he hears something, like if somebody is knocking on our door, if a smoke alarm goes off, or even if my baby brother is crying. When Barkley hears something, he nudges me and then leads me to where the sound is coming from. Barkley and I make a good team!

DEAFNESS SHOULD NOT BE AN OBSTACLE

There are many people in the world whose deafness didn't stop them from doing what they wanted to do. Did you know that Thomas Edison, one of America's great inventors, was hearing impaired? So was Beethoven, a famous music composer. There are even actors and actresses on television and in the movies who are deaf too!

One day I'm going to do something important too! Maybe I'll become a doctor or a lawyer, or maybe I'll invent something like Thomas Edison did. Mom always says that just because my ears need extra help to hear, it doesn't mean that the rest of me is impaired too. And being deaf is no excuse for not trying to be the best I can be!

THE REST OF MY BODY IS OK!

A GREAT FUTURE!

Mom's right! Before I figured it out,
I tried to avoid doing things by saying
that I couldn't because I was deaf.
It took me ten years to understand
that being deaf shouldn't stand in
my way of doing all the things I want
to do, like making friends, having fun,
and dreaming about the future!

Activities

CARTOON STRIPS

A cartoon strip is a number of different pictures in a row that tell a story. Not all cartoon strips use words to tell the story, but rather they use a sequence of pictures that change slightly from one picture box to the next. People who use sign language or lip reading to communicate with others need to be very observant. That means to be able to watch something very carefully. Being able to find the meaning of a cartoon strip that does not use words to tell the story can be quite tricky unless you are observant!

So let's see how good we are at finding the meaning of a story simply by being observant. Let's create our very own cartoon strip without using words to tell the story. To get started you will need construction paper or blank paper, pencil, ruler, crayons, and marker pens.

With the help of your ruler, divide your piece of paper into six boxes. Hint: Draw two lines of equal distance apart along the width of the paper and one line lengthwise down the center of the paper.

You are now ready to begin drawing your cartoon. Remember, as you move from one box to the next, your picture should show some kind of progression from one action to another. For example, in the first box I could draw a picture of a monkey on a ladder trying to pick an apple from a tree. In the next box, I could draw the monkey on the ground and the ladder fallen over. This tells the reader that the monkey fell off the ladder to the ground. The following boxes will tell the rest of the story and what happens to the monkey. Be creative, have fun, and don't forget to make your cartoon as funny and colorful as you can.

Show your cartoon to your family and friends and let's see how good they are at knowing what your story is about just from looking at the pictures!

COMMUNICATION CHARADES

Everybody loves charades! It's not only a lot of fun but it's also a great way to learn how to communicate without saying a word.

Let's play a game of charades and only use sign language and lip reading to communicate to the other players.

To get started you will need construction paper, scissors, glue, markers or crayons, stickers (optional), and a timer. Please ask your parents to go to the website https://www.startasl.com/american-sign-language-alphabet/ or https://deafchildren.org/2019/06/free-asl-alphabet-chart/ or https://frdat.niagara.edu/assets/Disability-Handouts/ASL-alphabet.pdf and download a copy of the sign language alphabet that you will need to play the game.

Cut the construction paper into at least 10-15 rectangular pieces approximately 3x5 inches. These are going to be our charade cards. Draw a picture of an animal, person, place, or thing on one side of the charade card. Write the name of your object under each picture. Decorate the other side or back of the charade card, with colorful designs, polka dots, or even some fancy stickers. Then you are ready to play.

Each player takes a turn by choosing a charade card from the top of the pile of cards. The object of the game is to communicate to the other players the picture that is on your card. You can either use sign language or say the word by moving your mouth, but DO NOT make a sound. The players will either have to use their sign language alphabet sheet or read your lips in order to guess the answer. You have two minutes to guess correctly! The player who guesses the correct answer gets a point. The player with the most points WINS! Have fun and charades away!

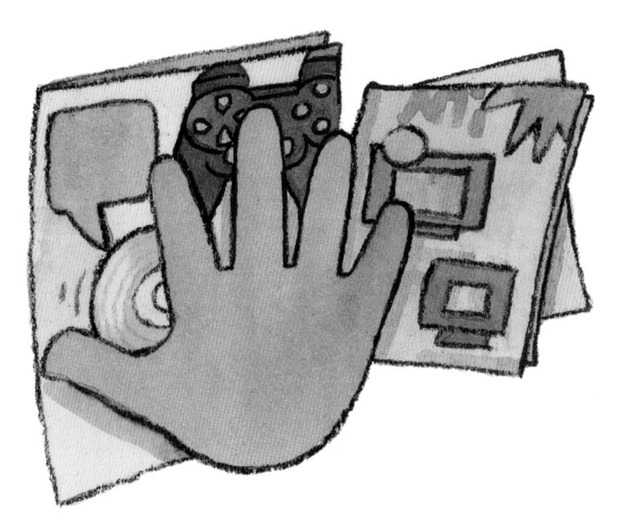

HANDPRINT COLLAGE

Collages are made from many overlapping pictures. Most collages use pictures that reflect a theme. For example a collage with an animal theme will have many overlapping pictures of different kinds of animals. Let's create a collage that helps us see all the ways we use our ears. For example, we use our ears when we listen to the television and the radio. How many other things can you find?

To begin you will need some construction paper, scissors, glue, old magazines or newspapers, pencil, crayons, and marker pens.

First trace your hand onto a piece of construction paper. Cut out your traced hand. Find pictures in old magazines, newspapers, or your own drawings that you want to include in your collage. Glue the pictures, overlaping them, to your construction paper hand. How many things did you find that you use your ears for?

Now let's make another handprint collage of all the things that a person who is deaf can use even though they can not hear. For example, a person who is deaf can still watch television, but instead of listening to the show, they read the writing at the bottom of their screen that tells them what is being said.

Can you think of some other things that a person who is deaf can use even though they are unable to hear? After you have completed both handprint collages, perhaps you have noticed that people who are deaf still use many of the same things that people who can hear use, but just in a different way.

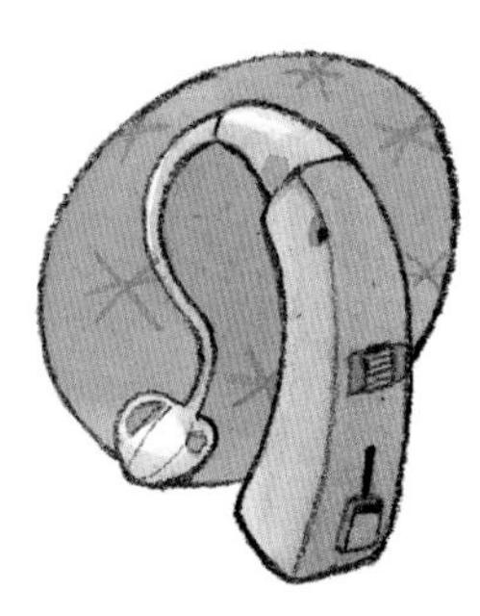

Parent's guide

The purpose of this book is to acknowledge the existence of deafness and hearing impairment among children while exploring some of the realities as well as resources available to individuals who are hearing impaired.

It is hoped that this book will promote a better understanding and acceptance of children who have any level of hearing impairment by eliminating any existing stigma.

Did you know that according to the National Institute on Deafness and Other Communication Disorders, 2 to 3 out of every 1,000 children in the United States are born deaf or hard-of-hearing, and 9 out of every 10 children who are born deaf are born to parents who can hear?

Approximately 28 million Americans have hearing loss. Hearing loss affects approximately 17 in 1,000 children under the age of 18 years.

Ten million Americans have suffered irreversible noise induced hearing loss and 30 million more are exposed to dangerous noise levels each day.

Only 1 out of 5 people who could benefit from a hearing aid actually wears one. This may be due to the stigma, perceived or real, attached to those individuals who are hearing impaired.

Recognizing behaviors in children that indicate hearing loss or impairment may be difficult at birth unless there is some type of obvious irregularity in regard to the ear. However, as your baby grows you may notice some behaviors which could indicate a problem with their hearing. For example, does your baby respond to your voice or turn toward other sounds within a room? Does your baby respond or get startled by loud noises such as the clapping of your hands? Or when your child gets to the age in which you would expect them to be talking, are they able to pronounce most of their words correctly? Children with hearing loss will often have difficulty saying simple words, such as *HI*, correctly, primarily because they are not able to hear the word properly when it is being said to them.

If you suspect that your child is experiencing any level of difficulty hearing, you may want to consider speaking to your family physician about having a formal hearing test completed in order to determine if hearing loss or impairment is apparent. Keep in mind that although these characteristics may indicate difficulty with your child's hearing, there could be other reasons why your child is displaying these symptoms. If you have any concerns, consult your family physician.

If you discover that your child has a significant hearing deficit, try not to panic. There are many treatments, support systems, and even technology that can help your child live a happy and productive life. Exploring the resources within your community in order to determine what is available to you and your child is a good place to start. Early intervention is important as hearing loss can affect a child's ability to develop speech, language and social skills. Participation in early intervention programs can help improve a child's overall development.

As a result of the continuous evolution and improvements with technology, individuals with hearing impairments have more options available to them. Options include: Behind the Ear Hearing Aids, Receiver in the Ear Hearing Aids, In the Ear Hearing Aids, Bone Conduction Hearing Device, Contralateral Routing of Sound Hearing Aids, Remote Microphone System, and Cochlear Implants. Other assistive devices include Frequency Modulation Systems, Captioning, Text Messaging, Telephone Amplifiers, Flashing and Vibrating Alarms, Audio Loop Systems, Infrared Listening Devices, Portable Sound Amplifiers, and Text Telephone or Teletypewriters.

First published in the United States in 2009 by BES and Gemser Publications.

c/ Castell, 38; Teià 08329 (Barcelona) – Spain (World Rights)
Website: www.gemserpublications.com
E-mail: merce@mercedesros.com
Illustrator: Marta Fàbrega
Author: Jennifer Moore-Mallinos

Published by Sourcebooks eXplore, an imprint of Sourcebooks
P.O. Box 4410, Naperville, Illinois 60567-4410
(630) 961-3900
sourcebookskids.com

Cataloging-in-Publication Data is on file with the Library of Congress.

Source of Production: HeShan Astros Printing Ltd. Industrial Development Area Xijiang River, Gulao Town, HeShan, GuangDong, China.
Date of Production: June 2022

Printed and bound in China.

LEO 10 9 8 7 6 5 4 3 2 1